Facts About
Planes

DONNA BAILEY

STECK-VAUGHN
LIBRARY
Austin, Texas

How to Use This Book

This book tells you many things about planes. There is a Table of Contents on the next page. It shows you what each double page of the book is about. For example, pages 14 and 15 tell you about "Engines for Planes."

On most of these pages you will find some words that are printed in **bold** type. The bold type shows you that these words are in the glossary on pages 46 and 47. The glossary explains the meaning of some words that may be new to you.

At the very end of the book there is an index. The index tells you where to find information about certain words in the book. For example, you can use the index to look up words like supersonic, jet engines, airlines, or anything else to do with planes.

Published in the United States in 1990 by Steck-Vaughn Co., Austin, Texas, a subsidiary of National Education Corporation.

© Macmillan Children's Books 1988
Artwork © BLA Publishing Limited 1988

All rights reserved. No reproduction, copy or transmission of this publication may be made without written permission.

Material used in this book first appeared in Macmillan World Library: *Travel by Air*. Published by Macmillan Children's Books.

Printed and bound in the United States
1 2 3 4 5 6 7 8 9 LB 94 93 92 91 90

Library of Congress
Cataloging-in-Publication Data
Bailey, Donna.
　Planes.

　(Facts about)
　Summary: Discusses how planes fly, the history of flight, the first airlines, occupations involving aeronautics, contemporary commercial flights, and other aspects of planes.
　1. Aeronautics—Juvenile literature. 2. Airplanes—Juvenile literature. [1. Aeronautics. 2. Airplanes]
　I. Title II. Series.
TL547.B32 1989   629.13   89-21737
ISBN 0-8114-2503-7

Contents

Big and Small Planes	4	Passengers	28
How Planes Fly	6	Air Cargo	30
Early Planes	8	Airport Safety	32
Early Flights	10	Into the Air	34
The First Airlines	12	Taking Off	36
Engines for Planes	14	Above the Clouds	38
Different Jobs	16	Landing	40
Planes Today	18	Supersonic Planes	42
On the Flight Deck	20	Looking Ahead	44
Planning a Flight	22		
Airlines of the World	24	Glossary	46
Cabin Staff	26	Index	48

 **Big and Small Planes**

Traveling by plane helps us get to faraway places very quickly.

Planes carry both people and **cargo**. Some planes are large and some are small.

The big plane in this picture can carry people on its two top decks, and cargo in the lower part of the plane.

Heathrow Airport, London

There are many different planes from many different countries at this airport in London.

In some countries, doctors fly small planes to help people like this man with a broken leg.

the doctor at work

How Planes Fly

A plane's engine pushes it forward. Air pushing against the plane makes **drag** and slows it down.

The wings **lift** the plane in the air. Its **weight** pulls it to the ground.

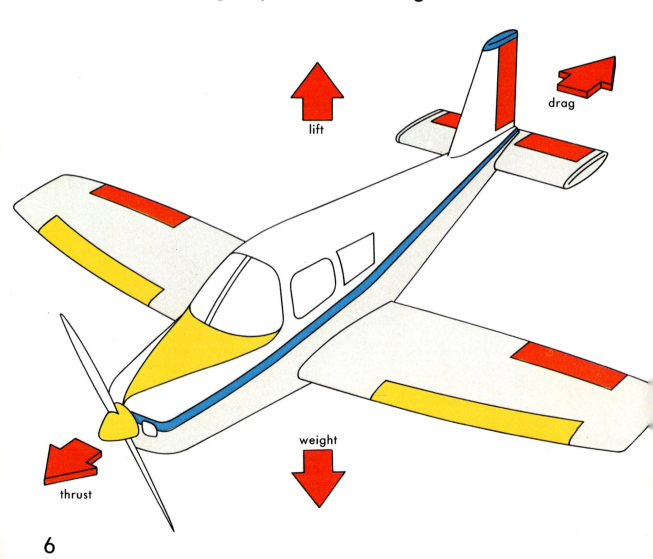

the shape of an airplane's wing

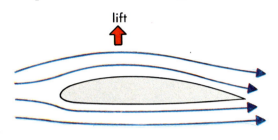

how planes change direction

A plane's wings are a special shape to give it more lift.

A plane has **elevators** to make it go up or down. **Ailerons** help it turn left or right.

A **pilot** uses the ailerons and the **rudder** to make the plane curve gently to the left or right.

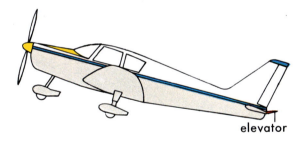

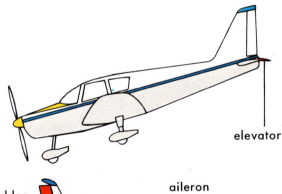

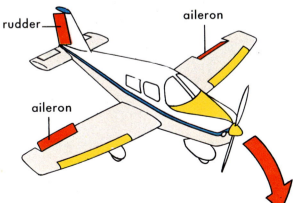

Early Planes

About 100 years ago planes did not have engines. They were **gliders** with big wings, which helped them stay in the air.

Our picture shows Otto Lilienthal. He built the first hang glider. He flew the glider by hanging under the wings, and changed direction by twisting his body.

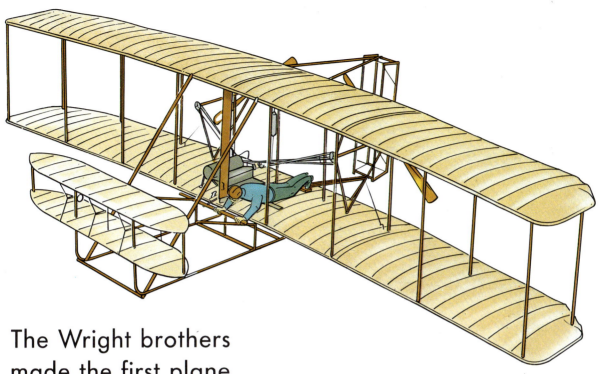

The Wright brothers made the first plane with an engine, called *Flyer 1*. Our photograph shows its first flight.

***Flyer I*, the first plane to have an engine**

Orville Wright on *Flyer I*

Early Flights

John Alcock and Arthur Brown were the first people to fly across the Atlantic, in 1919.

In 1927, Charles Lindbergh was the first person to fly **solo** from New York to Paris, in his plane, *The Spirit of St. Louis*.

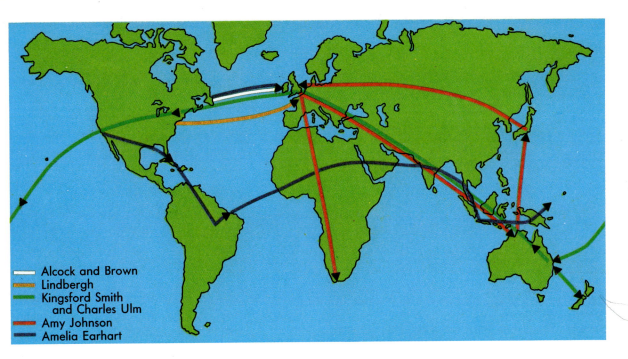

Our map shows some early flights.

Kingsford Smith and Charles Ulm were the first people to fly across the Pacific.

Amy Johnson was the first to fly solo from England to Australia.

Amelia Earhart tried to fly around the world, but crashed over the Pacific.

early flights

Some Important Dates in Air Travel

1891	Lilienthal flew his glider
1903	*Flyer I*'s first flight
1919	First Atlantic crossing
1928	First Pacific crossing
1930	First flight to Australia

The First Airlines

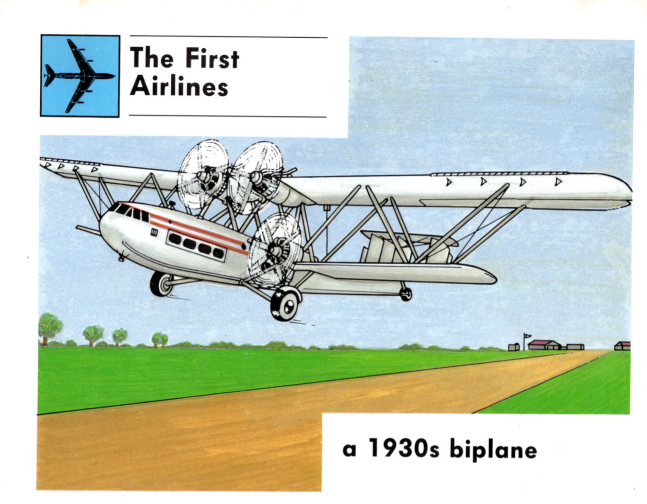

a 1930s biplane

Soon many people wanted to fly.
Larger planes were built
that could carry passengers
and mail.
   At first people flew **biplanes** with
four engines, like the one in our picture.
Then **airlines** started the first
flights that flew regular trips between
the United States and Europe.

Some airlines used **flying boats** that could land on water.

The DC3 was another popular plane, which is still in use.

a flying boat

the popular DC3

Engines for Planes

Planes now had more powerful engines with **propellers**.

When the propellers spin around they force the air backward, making a fast stream of air. This stream pushes the plane forward.

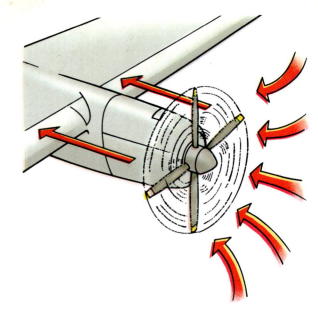

propellers are like fans

the air stream pushes the plane forward

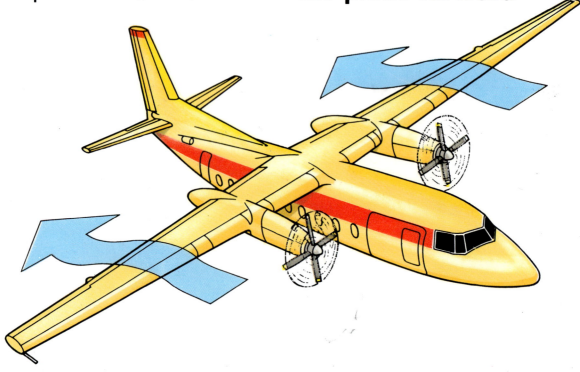

Then people invented jet engines. In a jet engine, a fan at the front of the engine sucks in cold air. The air inside the engine is packed very tight by more fans and it gets very hot.

The hot air is mixed with fuel and burns to give off very hot gases. These hot gases must escape so they rush out behind the engine in a stream, or jet. This jet pushes the plane forward.

in a jet engine cold air goes in at the front and a jet of hot gases comes out at the back

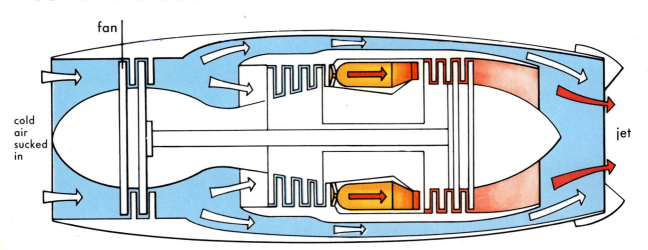

 **Different Jobs**

Planes today have many different shapes and sizes. People use planes for different jobs.

Our picture shows a small **jet** plane. Business people use it to visit customers in other cities.

Some people use planes to fight forest fires.

Farmers use planes to spray their crops and kill the pests. They also use planes to photograph their fields from the air.

Our table shows some small passenger planes that are built in different countries.

fighting a forest fire

A Selection of Small Passenger Aircraft					
Made by	Type	Country	Passengers	Speed (mph)	Range (miles)
De Havilland	Drover	Australia	8	158	900
G.A.F.	Nomad	Australia	15	193	840
De Havilland	Otter	Canada	11	160	876
Dassault	Falcon 10	France	7	568	2209
Israel Air Industries	Westwind	Israel	10	542	2870
Mitsubishi	MU-2	Japan	9	355	1606
Edgar Percival	EP9	United Kingdom	5	146	580
British Aerospace	BAe 125	United Kingdom	8	502	2683
Lockheed	Jetstar	United States	10	547	2994
Rockwell	Sabreliner	United States	10	563	1957
Gates Learjet	Learjet 35A	United States	8	534	2631
Beech	Super King Air	United States	13	333	1710
Antonov	AN-2	Soviet Union	14	160	559
Dornier	Skyservant	West Germany	13	202	654

Planes Today

Jet planes today are built to carry many passengers quickly and cheaply. The picture on the next page shows the shapes of some different jets.

The Boeing 747 on this page has a wide body and a large upper deck. It can carry many people. The 747 has four engines under the wings.

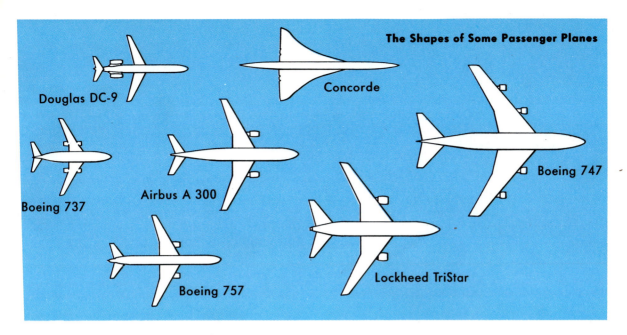

The back edges of a plane's wing have **flaps** and **spoilers**.

At **take off**, the pilot makes the flaps stretch out. This makes the wing bigger and gives the plane more lift. When landing, the pilot lowers the flaps and raises the spoilers to help slow the plane down.

the edge of a wing

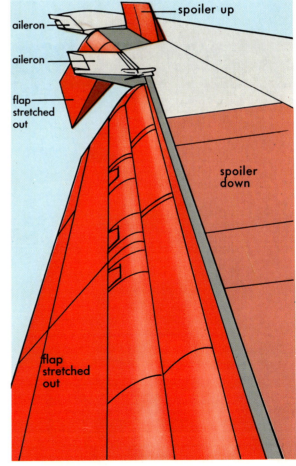

On the Flight Deck

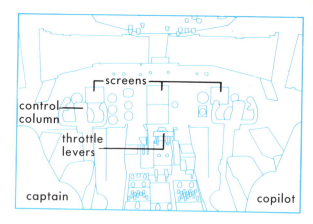

where the crew sits

Our picture shows the flight deck and controls of a plane. The captain always sits in the seat on the left.

The captain or the copilot flies
the plane and changes direction
by moving the control column.
Dials in front of them show the
plane's height, speed, and direction.
The **throttle levers** control the
power and speed of the engine.

The **engineer** sits behind the captain
and copilot. He tells the captain and copilot
how much **fuel** is being used during
the flight. He makes sure the engines
are working well.

# Planning a Flight

Before a flight, the **ground crew** checks to be sure that all parts of the plane are working properly.

The **flight plan** is worked out. This shows the **destination, route,** fuel, and number of passengers.

At the **flight center,** the captain checks the flight plan, the weather report, and his **flight path.** He tells his crew about the flight.

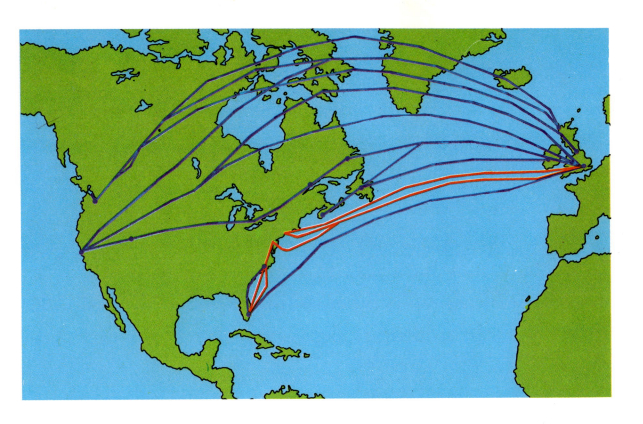

A flight path is a corridor in the air that keeps planes apart and makes sure they do not collide in midair.

Our map shows the Atlantic flight paths. The red lines show the flight paths for the fastest planes.

checking a jet engine

Airlines of the World

Airlines fly regular flights to all the countries in the world. There are about 500 airlines. Some countries have their own airlines.

Our pictures show 18 well-known airlines with their different **emblems** and colors. How many do you know?

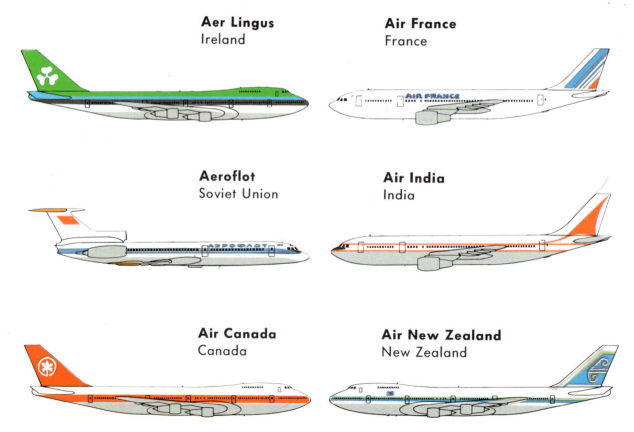

Aer Lingus
Ireland

Air France
France

Aeroflot
Soviet Union

Air India
India

Air Canada
Canada

Air New Zealand
New Zealand

Cabin Staff

The cabin staff looks after the passengers. They welcome the passengers on board, help them find their seats, and serve them food and drinks.

On long international flights, the cabin staff are busy all the time.

In our picture a **stewardess** is serving a meal to a passenger. She has just given the little boy a board game to play with his mother.

Passengers can read, watch movies, or listen to music, but many just want to sleep.

The cabin staff makes sure everybody is comfortable. They take care of anyone who is not feeling very well.

 # Passengers

getting on the plane

Passengers sometimes get on a plane by both the front and rear doors.

Our diagram shows a Boeing 747 that has three levels: a lower cargo deck, a main passenger deck, and a top deck for the more expensive seats.

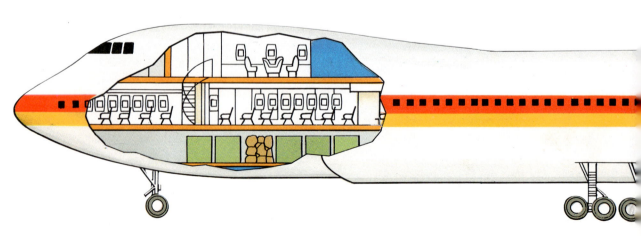

A Boeing 747 has ten seats in each row and two **aisles** so that people can walk around.

Flyer 1 flew 131 feet, less than half the length of a 747.

passengers on board a Boeing 747

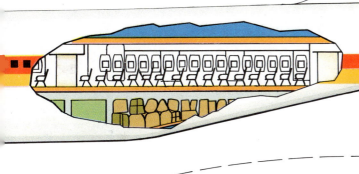

Air Cargo

Planes that carry cargo have rollers or rails in the floor. The cargo is often packed in large metal boxes called **containers**.

loading a container

inside the cargo hold

Cargo planes do not have seats. They carry goods in the cargo hold. The nose of the Boeing 747 in our picture lifts up to load the cargo.

Planes can carry cars, trucks, and animals as well as big containers.

This plane has an unusual cargo. It has a space shuttle on its back.

loading a Boeing 747

an unusual cargo

Airport Safety

Hundreds of people travel by air every day, so it is important for the airport officials to make sure that they can travel in safety.

Before getting on a plane, passengers pass through safety checks to make sure no one is carrying anything that is dangerous.

Passengers' baggage is also checked before the ground crew loads it onto the plane.

**checking the plane
clearing the snow**

Ground crews check the planes before they take off to make sure they work perfectly.

Snowplows clear the **runways** of snow.

Ambulances and fire engines are always ready if needed.

Into the Air

Controllers in the **control tower** tell the captain when the plane can take off. A **tractor** pulls the plane out from the **terminal building** and the captain **taxis** slowly forward onto the runway.

inside the control tower

leaving the terminal

At many airports, passengers board the planes by a corridor, so they do not get wet or cold.

This corridor is on wheels. Ground crews wheel the corridor away from the plane before the captain taxis out onto the runway.

If the airport is very busy, the planes wait in a line on the runway before they can take off.

Taking Off

Before take off, the captain releases the brakes and applies full power to the engines.

The plane races along the runway, gathering speed until the captain raises the **nose wheel** off the ground.

Our picture shows a Boeing 747 about to take off.

When the nose wheel is off the ground, the **landing wheels** leave the ground very quickly, and the plane climbs steeply upward.

Passengers can see the ground far below as the plane gets higher and turns onto its **course**.

about to take off

the plane is climbing steeply

 ## Above the Clouds

Planes fly very high, often above the clouds, because the air is thinner and the planes use less fuel. The flights are also smoother.

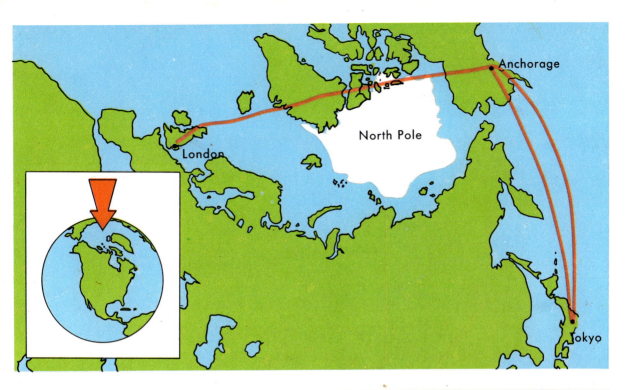

Our map shows the route planes take over the North Pole.

The captains find their way by **radio signals** from **beacons** on the ground.

Controllers along the route watch the planes on their **radar** screens and check that the planes are going the right way.

directing air traffic

The controllers tell the captains how high and how fast to fly.

They check that all planes are a safe distance apart.

 # Landing

When landing, the captain puts the plane into a shallow dive to lose speed. The captain lines up the plane with the runway and lets down the landing wheels. The flaps come out and the plane lands.

planes leave the stack to land

When lots of planes are waiting to land, the controllers put them in a **stack** above the airport.

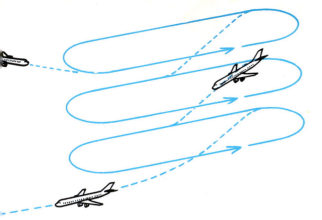

The planes circle around until it is their turn to land.

At night the runway lights are switched on so the captains can see the runway.

After landing, the ground crew uses batons to show the captain where to go.

the runway at night

signals to the captain

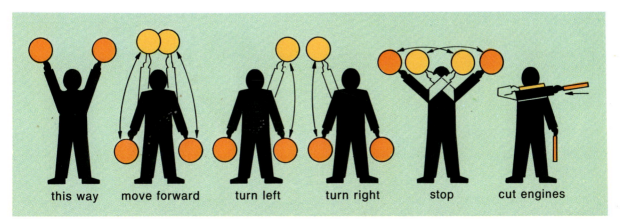

this way   move forward   turn left   turn right   stop   cut engines

Supersonic Planes

Planes that fly very fast have a shape like a dart. They have pointed bodies and swept back wings.

These planes fly so fast that they squash the air in front of them so that it builds up to form a barrier, called the sound barrier.

a supersonic plane breaking the sound barrier

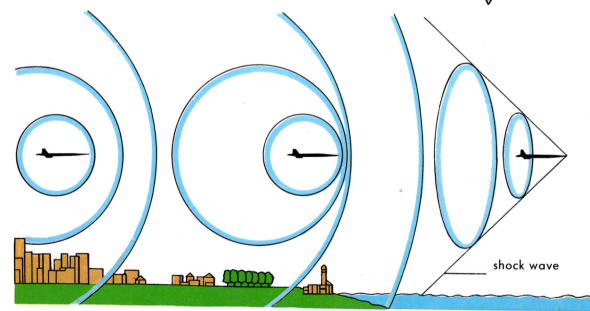

The plane bursts through the sound barrier, which causes a shock wave and makes a loud boom. Planes built to fly through the sound barrier are supersonic. They fly faster than the speed of sound.

Our picture shows the Concorde, the first supersonic airliner, built by the British and French. The Soviets have also built a supersonic airliner, the TU-144.

Looking Ahead

People are now designing different supersonic planes for use in the future.

One design looks like a future version of the Concorde. The one below looks more like a space shuttle.

a future Concorde?

a plane or a space shuttle?

People are also designing planes with wings that can fold away. These **"swing-wing"** planes can fly very fast.

The wings are used for landing and taking off, but fold back when the plane is at its cruising height. These planes are expensive to build, so it will be some time before we can fly in planes like these.

Glossary

aileron part of the wings that the pilot moves up and down when changing direction.

airline a company that flies planes from place to place at times fixed by a timetable.

aisle a passage for walking between rows of seats.

beacons towers on the ground that send out radio signals to planes.

biplanes a plane with two sets of wings, one above the other.

cargo the goods carried by a plane.

containers large metal boxes into which goods are packed to make them easier to move.

control tower the tall building at an airport where the controllers watch all the planes and tell the captains when to land or take off.

controllers people who control the movements of the planes when they are flying and tell the captains what to do.

course the direction a plane takes to get from one place to another.

destination the place where a plane is going.

drag air pushing against the plane, which slows it down as it flies.

elevators parts of the tail of a plane that the pilot moves up and down to make the plane go up or down.

emblem the badge of an airline.

engineer the person who takes care of the engines and other moving parts of the plane.

flaps parts at the back of the wing that the pilot moves to make the wing larger, or to slow the plane down.

flight center where all the planning for a flight is done.

flight path a "corridor" in the air that planes must fly along so that they keep safely apart from each other.

flight plan the written instructions to the captain about the flight.

flying boats planes that are able to land on water.

fuel the gasoline or kerosene used in the engine of the plane.

gliders planes without engines.

ground crew people at the airport who do all the jobs to make sure the planes fly safely.

jets planes with jet engines.
landing wheels wheels with large soft tires that the captain folds away after take off and puts down just before landing.
lift the air that flows around the wing and makes the plane go upward.
nose wheel the small wheel at the front of the plane that balances the plane when it is on the ground.
pilot the person who flies the plane.
propellers a propeller is made of two or more twisted blades. As it turns, it pulls a plane or ship along.
radar a way of finding an object when it cannot be seen. Radio signals are sent out and bounce off the object, back to the radar set. The radio waves make the object show up on a screen as a small "blip" of light.
radio signals signals sent out by a plane to tell the air traffic controllers where the plane is.
route the direction a plane flies in.
rudder the part of a plane's tail that the pilot moves to steer the plane.
runway the long flat wide road at an airport that planes take off from and land on.
solo alone, with no other person to help.
spoilers moving parts at the back of a plane's wing that are used as brakes to slow the plane down.
stack a group of planes circling above an airport waiting to land. A plane joins the stack at the top and gradually circles lower and lower until it is allowed to land.
stewardess a member of the cabin staff who looks after the passengers.
swing-wing planes planes with wings that fold back to make them smaller.
take off leaving the ground.
taxi when a plane travels slowly along the ground.
terminal building the building where passengers board their planes.
throttle levers the levers that change the speed of the engine so the plane flies faster or more slowly through the air.
tractor a special sort of vehicle that pulls the aircraft out of the terminal building.
weight how heavy something is.

Index

ailerons 7, 19
air 6, 14, 15, 38
airlines 12, 13, 24
aisles 29
Alcock, John, 10, 11

beacons 39
biplanes 12
Boeing 747 18, 28, 29, 31
Brown, Arthur 10, 11

cabin staff 26, 27
cargo 4, 28, 30, 31
Concorde 43, 44
containers 30, 31
control tower 34
controllers 34, 39, 40
controls 20, 21
crew 20, 22
crop spraying 17

DC3 13
doctors 5

Earhart, Amelia 11
elevators 7
engineers 21

fire fighting 17
flaps 19, 40
flight center 22
flight deck 20
flight plan 22
Flyer 1 9, 11, 29
flying boats 13
fuel 21, 22

gliders 8
ground crew 22, 32-33, 35, 41

jet engines 15
jet planes 16, 18
Johnson, Amy 11

landing wheels 37, 40
Lilienthal, Otto 8, 11
Lindbergh, Charles 10

nose wheel 36, 37

passenger planes 17
photography 17
pilot 7, 19
propellers 14

radar 39
radio signals 39
route 22, 39
rudder 7
runway 33, 34, 35 36, 40, 41

safety 32, 33
seats 28, 29, 31
Smith, Kingsford 11
solo flights 10, 11
sound barrier 42, 43
space shuttle 31, 44
spoilers 19
stack 40–41
supersonic planes 43, 44
swing-wing planes 45

take off 19, 36, 37
terminal building 34
throttle levers 21
TU-144 43

Ulm, Charles 11

weight 6
wings 6, 7, 8, 19, 42, 45
Wright brothers 9

Acknowledgments
The Publishers wish to thank the following organizations for their invaluable assistance in the preparation of this book: Australian Information Service, London; British Airports Authority; British Coledonian; Boeing Company; Cathay Pacific Airways; Civil Aviation Authority; KLM Royal Dutch Airlines; Lockheed — California Company; McDonnell Douglas; Royal Air Force Museum.
Photographic credits (t=top b=bottom l=left r=right)
Cover photograph: Colorific/Shelley Kotz. Title page; Colorific/Phillip Hoysar; 4, 5t Flight International; 5b Australian Information Service, London; 9 Flight International; 10 RAF Museum; 13t James Gilbert; 13b McDonnell Douglas; 16 DPR Marketing and Sales; 17 RAF Museum; 18, 20 Boeing Company; 21 Civil Aviation Authority; 22 KLM Royal Dutch Airlines; 23 British Airways; 26t British Caledonian; 26b British Airways; 27 Cathay Pacific; 28 ZEFA; 29 British Caledonian; 30t KLM Royal Dutch Airlines; 30b McDonnell Douglas; 31t British Airports Authority; 31b ZEFA; 32 British Airports Authority; 33t KLM Royal Dutch Airlines; 33b British Airports authority; 34t ZEFA; 34b, 35, 36 British Caledonian; 37t DPR Marketing and Sales; 37b Flight International; 38 Boeing Company; 39 ZEFA; 40 Flight International; 41 British Airports Authority; 43 Civil Aviation Authority; 44t, 45 Lockheed — California Company.